Jeffrey
The Big Horse with a Small Problem

A horse is transformed by the power of love.

By Lisa Brewer
Illustrated by Jean Abernethy

Jeffrey The Big Horse with a Small Problem
Book I of the Jeffi-Pooh Chronicles

Published by Inspired Touch Equine Services
P.O. Box 7
Lovettsville, Virginia 20180
www.inspiredtouchequine.com

Copyright © 2011 by Lisa Brewer

ISBN: 978-0-9832479-0-6

All rights reserved. No part of this book may be reproduced or transmitted in any form or by any means, electronic, mechanical, photocopying, recording or otherwise, without the prior written permission of the copyright owner.

*To my sister, Susan,
who is raising two
beautiful girls with a love
for animals.*

The school year was over. Amelia and Isabelle liked to spend the summers with their Aunt Lisa on her horse farm.

In past years, Amelia and Isabelle got to ride their aunt's old horse, Blake. But this year, there was a new horse. His name was Jeffrey.

Jeffrey was a big, strong, brown horse. He had a black mane and tail and a white blaze down his face. He was handsome, but something wasn't quite right. This horse had a mean, hard look in his eye. Jeffrey was an angry horse.

Jeffrey was so angry that he often chased Blake around the field. Jeffrey kicked and he bucked.

Sometimes, he even tried to bite Blake.

Aunt Lisa had to put Blake in one field and Jeffrey in another. She had to separate them so that Blake would not be frightened.

The day before Amelia and Isabelle were to arrive, Aunt Lisa took Jeffrey to a horse trainer.

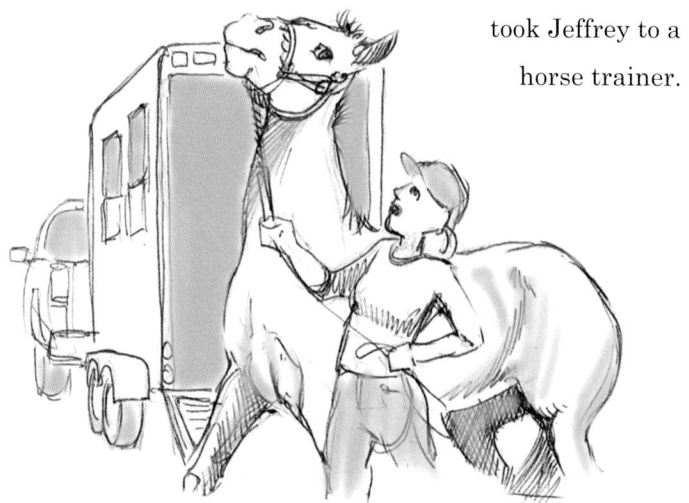

Jeffrey was nervous about being in a new place. He was so nervous he held his head high and his eyes wide open.

Aunt Lisa tried to help him relax, but that just made Jeffrey angry. He tried to buck her off!

All of a sudden, the trainer burst out and said, "Yuk! That horse of yours is no good." Then, she stuck her tongue out at Jeffrey!

Upon returning home, Aunt Lisa put Jeffrey out in the field behind the barn. She was feeling sad because Jeffrey tried to buck her off. Even the horse trainer said he was no good.

She decided Jeffrey could stay in the field and graze. No one would want to spend time trying to ride an angry horse.

Amelia and Isabelle arrived the next morning. They were very excited to meet the new horse. They barely said hello to their aunt before they asked if they could see Jeffrey.

As soon as Amelia set eyes on Jeffrey she immediately yelled, "Aunt Lisa, Aunt Lisa, can I ride him now?" Aunt Lisa knew that Amelia was a good rider but she had to tell her, "No."

Amelia and Isabelle looked disappointed as they sat down on a bale of hay nearby.

Their aunt explained, "Girls listen. Jeffrey is not the nicest horse. He gets mad and tries to buck the rider off. So, you can visit with Jeffrey, but you are not allowed to ride him."

Over the next week, Amelia spent hours with Jeffrey. Each day, she brushed him and talked to him. She picked grass and fed it to him from her hand. They became friends.

Amelia said to him, "I like you so much Jeffrey. I think you are the greatest horse that ever lived."

Each evening the girls would help feed the horses. Amelia would give her favorite horse a treat. She believed Jeffrey was a good horse even though he didn't always act like it.

One night, Amelia asked her aunt again if she could ride Jeffrey. "Please, Aunt Lisa. I just know he will be good with me." Her aunt said, "Sorry Amelia, the answer is still no. But, you can ride Blake anytime you want."

The next day, Amelia and Isabelle were out near the barn. Amelia put a halter on Jeffrey and walked him over to the fence. Isabelle looked at her sister and asked, "What are you doing?" Amelia said, "I'm going to ride him. Are you going to tell?" Isabelle said, "No, I won't tell."

Amelia climbed the fence and jumped on Jeffrey's back.

She rode him around the paddock. Then, she asked Isabelle to open the gate to the pasture. Isabelle said, "I don't want to get in trouble."

At that time, Aunt Lisa was doing the dishes. She looked out the kitchen window and saw Amelia riding Jeffrey.

She ran out the door and yelled, "Amelia, get down off that horse right now!" Amelia said, "But Aunt Lisa, I told you he was good with me."

Her aunt said, "Amelia, please get down." Amelia threw her leg over the horse's back and slid to the ground.

"Amelia, you knew you were not allowed to ride that horse. What do you think should happen now?" Amelia scrunched her face and said, "Discipline?" "Yes." her aunt responded. "And, what do you think the discipline should be?" Amelia said, "I don't know."

"Tomorrow you will spend the afternoon picking up horse poop." Her aunt continued, "After that, we will talk about the horse."

The next afternoon, Amelia picked up a lot of manure.

But, she didn't mind because Jeffrey was there to keep her company. Sometimes he would give her a friendly nudge as she walked by.

That night at dinner, Aunt Lisa said, "Okay, let's talk about the horse."

Amelia said, "He is so good with me just like I told you he would be." "Amelia," Aunt Lisa replied, "I can see this is important to you so maybe we can find a way for you to ride Jeffrey." "YEAH!" Amelia yelled.

The next day, her aunt put Jeffrey on a lunge line and let Amelia ride him with her guidance. He really was good with her. Within two weeks, Amelia was allowed to ride Jeffrey by herself. She rode him every day for the next month.

Amelia asked her aunt if she could ride Jeffrey in a horse show. Her aunt replied, "There is a small horse show just down the road this weekend." Amelia shouted, "YIPEE!" Aunt Lisa said, "Now wait a minute.

We will take Jeffrey to the horse show. But, if he is too nervous about being in a new place, you will not ride him there." Amelia said, "He won't be too nervous."

That weekend, at the horse show, Jeffrey seemed to be relaxed.

Aunt Lisa thought to herself, "Maybe all those encouraging words from Amelia helped Jeffrey's confidence."

Amelia rode
Jeffrey well
in the show.
Jeffrey won first place.

Amelia hugged Jeffrey and said, "I knew you could do it. Now everyone can see you are a good horse."

The very next weekend, Aunt Lisa took Amelia and Jeffrey to another horse show. Only this time, it was a big show where all the best horses and riders were entered.

Jeffrey won first place at that show too. The horse trainer that stuck her tongue out at Jeffrey was also there. She saw Jeffrey win first place!

The horse trainer asked Aunt Lisa, "What did you do to make Jeffrey so good?" "I didn't do anything." Aunt Lisa replied, "Amelia worked with Jeffrey."

The trainer turned to Amelia and asked her the same question. Amelia said, "It's simple really. I loved him. I spent time with him and I said good things about him." "That's it?" the trainer asked. Amelia replied, "Well, we practiced a lot too. But, mostly he is just a great horse."

Amelia knew Jeffrey was always a good horse on the inside. But everybody else could only see the way he acted on the outside. They didn't know the reason Jeffrey was so angry was because nobody loved him. But now, he was a good horse on the inside and on the outside.

He was even nice to Blake. The two horses were now friends. They would run and play together.

By the end of the summer, Jeffrey was doing so well that Isabelle was riding him too. He seemed to really enjoy the attention he got from the girls.

Amelia and Isabelle's mom came to pick them up. She asked, "What turned Jeffrey around from that angry horse to a happy, gentle horse?" Aunt Lisa said, "I learned from Amelia that sometimes you have to love someone before they can become lovely."

The girls' mom said, "Come on girls, we need to get going. Tell your Aunt Lisa, thank you."

Amelia and Isabelle thanked their aunt and gave her a big hug. Amelia said, "Aunt Lisa you have to promise you will love Jeffrey and say nice things to him." "I promise." Her aunt replied. I have to go say goodbye to Jeffrey now." Amelia said as she hurried away.

Amelia went out to see Jeffrey for the last time. She told him, "Jeffrey, you have to be good. I know you can do it. Aunt Lisa loves you too and she'll take care of you until I get back. I will miss you so much.

I'm glad you and Blake are friends now. He will keep you company."

Jeffrey nuzzled Amelia as if to say, "Thank you for being so kind to me."

Amelia and Isabelle got in the car with their mom to go home. But, before they left they told their aunt, "Jeffrey is cuddly as a pooh bear."

So, Aunt Lisa now calls him Jeffi-Pooh.

The Beginning

Questions for Young Readers

How could you tell Jeffrey was angry?

What was Jeffrey so angry about?

Why did the horse trainer think Jeffrey was no good?

Was the horse trainer right about Jeffrey?

Why should we never say bad things about others?

Do you think saying bad things about others can hurt their confidence?

What helped Jeffrey get over his anger?

For adults to read actual events of Jeffrey's story,

go to www.inspiredtouchequine.com

and click on Life Lessons

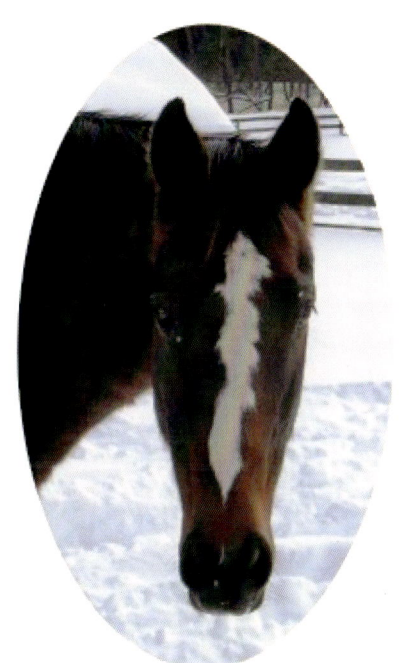

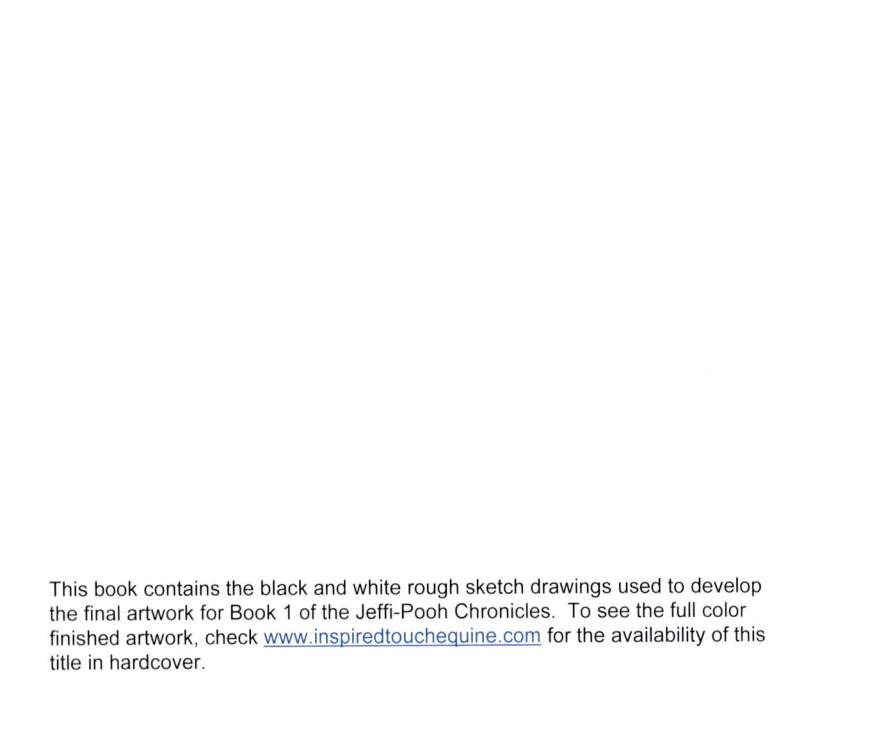

This book contains the black and white rough sketch drawings used to develop the final artwork for Book 1 of the Jeffi-Pooh Chronicles. To see the full color finished artwork, check www.inspiredtouchequine.com for the availability of this title in hardcover.